HO CHI MINH

PHILIP STEELE

Heinemann Library
Chicago, Illinois

Customer Service 888-454-2279

Visit our website at www.heinemannlibrary.com

Originated by Dot Gradations, Ltd.
Printed by South China Printing Company, Ltd.

07 06 05 04 03
10 9 8 7 6 5 4 3 2 1

Library of Congress Cataloging-in-Publication Data

Steele, Philip, 1948-
  Ho Chi Minh / Philip Steele.
     p. cm. -- (Leading lives)
Summary: A biography of the Vietnamese leader who led his people in the struggle for independence from France and in the subsequent war with South Vietnam and the United States.
Includes bibliographical references and index.
  ISBN 1-40340-836-X (HC)
  1. Háão, Châi Minh, 1890-1969--Juvenile literature. 2. Presidents--Vietnam (Democratic Republic)--Biography--Juvenile literature. [1. Háão, Châi Minh, 1890-1969. 2. Heads of state. 3. Vietnam--History--1945-1975.] I. Title. II. Series.
  DS560.72.H6 S74 2003
  959.704'092--dc21

2002012044

Acknowledgments
The author and publishers are grateful to the following for permission to reproduce copyright material: pp. 4, 15, 41, 45 Popperfoto; p. 7 Tim Page/Corbis; p. 9 Archivo Iconografico S.A./Corbis; p. 10 Steve Raymer/Corbis; pp. 12, 22 Hulton Deutsch Collection/Corbis; pp. 18, 37, 39, 47 Camera Press; pp. 20, 27, 32, 35, 49 Hulton Archive; pp. 25, 40, 43, 54 Bettmann/Corbis; pp. 26, 28 Peter Newark; pp. 50, 52 Steve Raymer/Corbis; p. 55 Macduff Everton/Corbis.

Cover photograph of Ho Chi Minh reproduced with permission of Hulton Archive.

Some words are shown in bold, **like this.** You can find out what they mean by looking in the glossary.

Contents

1 For Vietnam!

It was September 2, 1945. All morning, thousands of people, young and old, had poured into the city of Hanoi, in Vietnam. Merchants closed their shops and joined the excited crowds in the square. People carried flowers, and red flags and banners fluttered on every street.

A call for freedom

Shortly after 2:00 P.M., a thin, simply dressed man climbed up onto the public platform. He looked out over the sea of faces, the young men in white shirts, the village women in colorful robes. Some of the elderly men held ancient weapons from past wars.

The man on the platform was Ho Chi Minh, Vietnam's new leader. He declared that his country would no longer be ruled by the French or the Japanese. Long ago, he said, the French people had risen up against an unjust king, and people in the United States had rebelled against the rule of the British. They had declared that all people were born free and had equal rights. Vietnam, too, would now become an independent nation.

As Ho Chi Minh finished speaking and stepped down from the platform, he must have been looking back over his life and his long struggle to make this dream come true. He knew only too well that the struggle was far from over.

A man of his times

"Who is this man?" muttered some people in the crowd, as the cheers died down.

*◀ Ho Chi Minh spent all his adult life fighting for an independent, united **Communist** Vietnam.*

A declaration of freedom

"All the peoples on earth are equal from birth, all the peoples have the right to live, to be happy and free. . ."

(From the Vietnamese Declaration of Independence, 1945)

It was a good question. Ho Chi Minh was not well known to the people of Hanoi. For many years, he had led a secret life. He had changed his name several times and had lived in many different parts of the world.

During the next twenty years, however, the name of Ho Chi Minh would become famous not just in Southeast Asia, but around the world.

Ho Chi Minh lived in stormy times. At the time of his birth, in 1890, powerful European countries were extending their rule over most of the world. The struggle of those lands to regain their freedom would last his entire lifetime.

In the early 1900s, political systems that had been in place for hundreds of years were coming under attack. The Chinese had forced the emperor from power in 1911. The Russian people did the same to the czar in 1917. Between 1914 and 1918, the great powers of the day fought each other in World War I, with great loss of life.

Inspired by the Russian **Revolution,** Communists were calling for workers all over the world to seize power. Severe economic problems in the 1920s and 1930s allowed **dictators** to take over Italy, Germany, and Spain. World War II raged from 1939 to 1945, followed by the **Cold War** (1945–1991), a long period of tension between the United States and the Soviet Union. Ho Chi Minh was witness to and involved in many of these history-making events.

The Flier of Kites

Vietnam is a country in Southeast Asia, east of Laos and Cambodia. It is mountainous in the northwest, but in the east a hot, humid plain borders the blue waters of the South China Sea. Tropical forests and rice fields blanket much of the land. In the north, most Vietnamese people live along the Hong River, and in the south they live along the Mekong River.

Village boy

The man we know as Ho Chi Minh was born with the name Nguyen Sinh Cung on May 19, 1890. His birthplace was the village of Hoang Tru, near the city of Vinh. Although Vietnam still had its own emperor at that time, France governed it as part of a territory called Indochina.

As a little boy, Ho Chi Minh liked to fly his paper kite with his older brother and sister. His mother Hoang Thi Loan enjoyed singing and telling tales to her children.

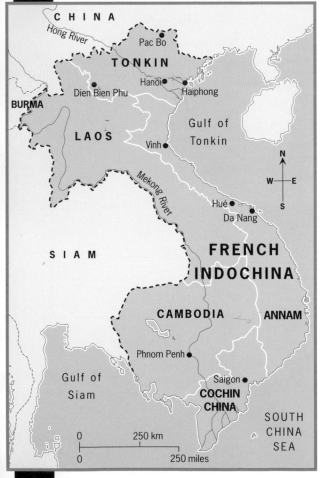

◀ This map shows Vietnam in 1890. There were three regions— Tonkin, Annam, and Cochin China. Together with Laos and Cambodia, they formed French-ruled Indochina.

▲ *Ho lived in this house in the village of Kim Lien after his mother's death in 1901.*

Sadness in the city

When Ho was five years old, his family moved south to the city of Hué, where his father Nguyen Sinh Sac was to study. Sadly, Ho's mother died there while giving birth to another baby in 1901. He and the other children had to return to Hoang Tru, where their grandmother cared for them until their father passed his exams.

When Nguyen Sinh Sac returned north, he was expected to take a job at the emperor's court. However, he refused, saying that he was too upset by his wife's death. Instead, he set up a little school in his home village of Kim Lien. He was an intelligent man, widely respected for his learning.

Key dates: Vietnam in the 1800s

1802	• Vietnam is united as a single empire
1859	• French capture the southern city of Saigon
1862	• French gain control of central Vietnam (known as Annam)
1867	• French gain control of southern Vietnam (known as Cochin China)
1874	• French invade northern Vietnam (known as Tonkin)
1885	• All Vietnam comes under French control
1887	• Laos, Cambodia, and Vietnam are united under French rule as Indochina

New ideas

Another reason existed for Nguyen's refusal of the job at the court. Like many of his friends, he had no respect for the royal court, which under French rule no longer had any real power. He was a **nationalist** who opposed French rule. He believed that his country had the right to rule itself. He also refused to speak French, which was necessary for anyone wishing to take an official job at this time. Interested in Vietnamese history and writing, he also wanted to learn more about European and American ideas and the modern world. Young Ho loved to hear his father arguing about politics and ideas and soon showed that he was a fast learner.

"One Who Will Succeed"

It was an old Vietnamese custom that boys were given a new name as a sign that they were growing up. At the age of eleven, Ho Chi Minh was given the name Nguyen Tat Thanh, which means "one who will succeed."

Teachers and lessons

Most teachers at that time expected children to learn their lessons by heart. But Ho's father and a family friend named Vuong Thuc Qui, a **nationalist** rebel, taught Ho for a time. They disliked teaching that just required the student to memorize facts. Instead, his father and Vuong taught young Ho to think for himself.

One of Ho's favorite books was an old Chinese story called *Journey to the West,* full of monsters, demons, and the fantastic adventures of a character named Monkey.

At the age of fifteen, Ho's father sent him to a school in Vinh, where he learned to speak French. Even nationalists agreed that they would never defeat France if the Vietnamese could not understand French.

The student rebel

The following year, Nguyen was again asked to work for the royal court as an official. He could not refuse this time without being marked as a rebel, so he traveled back to Hué with a heavy heart.

▶ *As a child, Ho studied the ideas of the Chinese **philosopher** Confucius (551–479 B.C.E.). China had ruled Vietnam in ancient times, and the Vietnamese still thought the teachings of Confucius were important.*

In 1907, Ho passed the entrance exam for the National Academy in Hué. Some rich students made fun of Ho for being a poor country boy. He took no notice, though, and studied hard, learning science and geography.

Life was hard for the country people of Indochina. In 1908, poor villagers poured into Hué, protesting high taxes. Ho joined them and offered to translate their demands into French. Authorities ordered the protesters to go away. When they refused, French troops fired upon them. The next day, the National Academy expelled Ho.

Heading south

It was the beginning of difficult times for Ho's whole family. The **imperial** security forces were persecuting them. Ho's father was moved to a job in a region 180 miles (290 kilometers) from Hué.

Ho himself went into hiding and then traveled south, working for a time as a teacher. In 1911, he ended up in Saigon and began to dream of leaving his homeland to find out more about the world.

◀ *Today, farmland still stretches beyond the old city walls of Hué, where peasants protested in 1908.*

4 Citizen of the World

In June 1911, 21-year-old Ho boarded a French steamer anchored in Saigon. The young man had registered under a false name, Van Ba. He was not to be a passenger, but a worker. The ship was about to sail to France and back.

TO LOCATE SAIGON, SEE THE MAP ON PAGE 6.

On leaving home
"I saw that I must go abroad to see for myself. After I had found out how they lived, I would return . . . to help my countrymen."

(Ho Chi Minh)

To France and back
Ho toiled day and night, scrubbing down the decks and carrying sacks of food for the cook. The seas were rough in the Indian Ocean, and the ship pitched and tossed. At last it passed through the Suez Canal into the Mediterranean Sea and finally docked at Marseille, in southern France.

Ho's first impressions of Europe were mixed. He was surprised to discover how many French people were poor, too. He also found that some were friendly toward him. Ho's ship then sailed north to Le Havre, before the return voyage to Vietnam.

The wanderer
Following his return, Ho did not stay long in Saigon. He began a period of wandering around the world. To pay for his travel, he worked on ships and took all kinds of jobs on shore.

He went back to France and then to the seaports of northern and western Africa, Arabia, India, and Madagascar. Wherever he traveled, the poverty of local people and the harshness of European colonial rule horrified him. Local people had no political rights and could not vote. Imprisonment was common, and punishments were often brutal. Employment was often little better than slavery, with terrible working conditions and little reward.

Ho also visited South America and in 1913 spent some time in the United States. He found odd jobs in New York City and Boston. The skyscrapers and modern technology astounded him, but the way in which whites treated the African Americans he met there saddened him.

▼ This photo shows New York City as it looked when Ho visited there in 1913. The city made a lasting impression on him.

Soon, Ho was in England. He worked in two well-known hotels in London, learning to be an assistant pastry chef. The amount of food wasted in the hotels shocked him, especially at a time when poor people were going hungry.

War years

World War I (1914–1918) broke out in August 1914. Ho soon realized that this would be war on a scale the world had never known before. The rulers of the world's biggest overseas empires—Great Britain, France, Germany, and Belgium—seemed to be locked into a fight to the bitter end. Surely this would also bring an end to their power? Ho thought perhaps the peoples they ruled would not have to fight for their freedom after all.

In 1917, Ho crossed the English Channel and settled in Paris. He found work as a photo retoucher. (In the days before color photography, people liked to have their black-and-white pictures tinted by hand.) In his spare time, he studied in libraries and improved his French language skills.

Ho saw that many other young Vietnamese were also now living in France. The French government had brought them over from the **colonies** to work in the factories because so many Frenchmen were away fighting in the war. With the other Vietnamese, he discussed the future of his homeland and the ways in which its people could become free.

The idealist

Ho read all the books he could find about the American and French **revolutions** that had taken place more than 200 years before. The **revolutionaries,** in their belief that all humans are born equal and in their shared ideals of freedom and justice, inspired him. Ho's travels had interested him in **social justice** and **human rights,** not just in Vietnam but around the world. He and his friends discussed the situation in China, where the **nationalist** Sun Zhongshan (sometimes called Sun Yat-sen) had overthrown the emperor in 1911, and in Russia, where a **Communist** revolution had taken place in November 1917.

The world seemed to be changing rapidly. However, when World War I ended in 1918, the European empires were still in place and seemed as powerful as ever.

Demands for change

In 1919, Ho and his friends set up a society called the Association of Annamese (Vietnamese) **Patriots.** The patriots drew up a list of demands for **democratic** reform. Ho signed the document "Nguyen Ai Quoc." He used this false name for many years to avoid detection by his enemies.

The leaders of Europe and the United States were gathering at this time in Versailles, near Paris, France, to draw up an

Demands of the patriots

- pardon and release for people imprisoned for their political views
- equal rights for all citizens
- freedom for newspapers, magazines, and radio
- freedom to hold meetings and organize political groups and trade unions to protect workers' pay and working conditions
- freedom to travel abroad
- a proper education system
- government by rule of law—elected representatives being sent to the French **parliament**

▲ *The world's leading powers met at Versailles in 1919 to plan the new world order.*

international **peace treaty.** Ho and his friends decided that this was a good time to **lobby** governments about the future of their country. They published their demands in the press and turned them over to members of the French parliament (law-making branch of the government) and to the French president himself.

They also gave their demands to the foreign politicians meeting at Versailles. Ho especially hoped that the United States would be sympathetic, because U.S. governments had often criticized the European-ruled empires. Surely the demands that he and his friends were making were just the same as the ones being put forward at the peace conference?

No reply

It seemed to Ho and his friends that the ideals of the United States and European nations did not apply to the peoples they ruled in distant parts of the world. The U.S. government thanked Ho for the document but took no action. The demands angered the French. They immediately set secret police agents on the trail of this "Nguyen Ai Quoc." Copies of the document arrived in Vietnam, and nationalist supporters passed them around.

5 The Red Flag

At the age of 30, Ho had glossy black hair and bright, intelligent eyes. It was now December 1920 and, dressed in a smart suit and tie, he was traveling to the French city of Tours. There, a group of French **socialists** were holding a big conference.

Ho had met many socialists since his return to France in 1917. These people hoped to create a new kind of society. This new society would be run by the working people rather than by **capitalists** (the people who grew rich by owning companies or by buying and selling **stock shares**).

Which way forward?
Some socialists believed that the best way to bring about their ideal world was to take part in the existing political system and call for reform or gradual change. Others declared that real change could only happen if workers all over the world rose up and seized power for themselves. Such **revolution** was the only way they thought they could change the whole economic and political system. Revolution was the way to create a fair society.

FOR DETAILS ON KEY PEOPLE OF HO CHI MINH'S TIME, SEE PAGE 58.

Ho became interested in these ideas. He read the books of the German political thinker Karl Marx (1818–1883) and of Vladimir Ilyich Lenin (1870–1924), the **Communist** who had led the revolution in Russia in November 1917. Ho came to realize that Vietnam needed a revolution to bring real freedom to the Vietnamese.

Talking in Tours
Ho arrived in Tours followed by the French government's secret agents, who were always on his trail. At the conference, he made quite an impression. Ho declared that the struggle

for freedom in lands such as Vietnam should be at the center of any socialist policy.

Many of the people there disagreed. They believed that the revolution would not be brought about by farmers growing rice in the villages of Asia, but by workers in the factories, mines, and steel mills of Europe and the United States.

At the end of the meeting in Tours, Ho voted for the founding of a new French Communist party that would be part of the Communist International (known as the **Comintern**). Communists in Moscow had set up Comintern in March 1919, with the aim of bringing together all the different Communist parties around the world.

Ho continued with his political **campaigns,** writing articles, and forming relationships with people from other **colonies.** He often had fierce arguments with other socialists. He was poor but still found time to enjoy himself in Paris, making many friends and visiting museums and galleries.

The land of revolution

In 1923, Ho sailed to Russia, which was renamed the Union of Soviet Socialist Republics, or Soviet Union, in 1922. Comintern invited him there to hear his views.

The Soviet Union was a whirlwind of activity and argument. These were exciting times, but everyday life was chaotic. The authorities even **detained** Ho for weeks before they gave him official permission to enter the country.

Moscow life

FOR DETAILS
ON KEY
PEOPLE OF
HO CHI
MINH'S TIME,
SEE PAGE 58.

At last he settled in Moscow. The **Communists** gave him work with the far eastern office of the **Comintern,** which was setting up contacts with Communists in China and Southeast Asia. He also studied at the university, where he met many people who would play an important part in history. Jiang Jieshi (Chiang Kai-Shek) was one of those people. He was a Chinese **nationalist** and a brilliant soldier who later became president of the Chinese republic. He proved to be extremely hostile to the Chinese Communists, but in the 1930s a Japanese invasion forced him to fight alongside the Communists.

◀ *The Chinese nationalist leader Sun Zhongshang, or Sun Yat-sen (right), is shown here in 1923 with Jiang Jieshi, or Chiang Kai-shek (left). Ho met both these future leaders in Moscow.*

Ho also met Zhou Enlai (Chou En-Lai). This Chinese Communist leader helped to bring about a victory in China and served as **prime minister** from 1949 to 1975.

Ho found himself having the same arguments in Moscow that he had in France. Many of his fellow Communists would not agree that freedom for people living in **colonies** such as Vietnam was an urgent part of the **revolution.** Some saw it as a side issue or as a later stage.

Marx and Lenin had said that a just society would be created only after the **working classes** in all countries were free. True national freedom would come only from international struggle. Ho agreed, but the injustices of his childhood in Vietnam were fresh in his mind. He could tell of overcrowded jails, of toil in the rubber **plantations,** of the way in which Europeans despised his people. To him, freedom for Vietnam and all the other European colonies was not only a just cause but a key part of any revolution.

The colonies count!

"Why do you neglect the colonies, while capitalism uses them to support itself, defend itself, and fight you?"

(Ho, in an address to the fifth Congress of the Comintern, 1924)

Ho longed to be back in his own part of the world. Since signing the list of demands drawn up by Vietnamese nationalists in Versailles, he could not return to Vietnam without being arrested by the French. But revolution was in the air in neighboring China, and he wanted to be part of it.

The Secret Agent

In October 1924, the **Comintern** sent Ho on a secret mission—to make contact with **revolutionaries** in China. The train steamed out of Moscow and crossed the Ural Mountains into the vast eastern wilderness of Siberia. Day after day, the train steamed through forests of birch and spruce and chugged through villages of wooden houses.

Even today a journey on the Trans-Siberian Railway can take a week. In 1924, it took three times as long. Mounted soldiers of the Red (Soviet) Army patrolled the line and checked travel permits. At last the train steamed into Vladivostok, the Soviet Union's chief port on the Pacific coast.

To Guangzhou

From there, Ho took a ship southward, following the coast of China. It docked amid the hooting steamships and wooden sailing vessels in the busiest harbor in southern China. The foreign traders based there called this great city Canton, but its Chinese name was Guangzhou.

In the early 1920s, much of China was in a state of chaos. The Chinese **nationalists** who had seized power in 1911 had not

▼ *A gunboat patrols Guangzhou harbor. The 1920s were troubled times in China.*

been able to keep control of the whole country. Regional **warlords** had seized power. In their efforts to rule all of China, the nationalists were now in alliance with the newly formed Chinese **Communist** party. Guangzhou was then the chief city of this alliance, and Ho was eager to make contact with people from both sides.

The port of Guangzhou lay just across the sea from Vietnam, and Ho found many other Vietnamese **exiles** in town. They each had different political plans for their homeland. Some were nationalists, and others were Communists. Some were even planning acts of terrorism.

TO LOCATE GUANGZHOU, SEE THE MAP ON PAGE 30.

Ho spread the ideas of Marx and Lenin and built up support for the Comintern. He also put these ideas into a weekly newspaper that was sent over to Vietnam, where anti-French feelings grew stronger every day.

Ho's time in Guangzhou was not just spent on politics. He also got married at this time, to a young woman named Tang Tuyet Minh. They liked each other well enough, but they had little in common. It soon became clear that the marriage was a mistake. She thought he was too old for her, and he could not interest her in his political dreams.

On the run

The alliance between Chinese nationalists and Communists had never been strong, and it was soon over. Sun Zhongshan had died, and the new leader of the nationalists was Jiang Jieshi. Ho had met him in Moscow. In March 1927, in the city of Shanghai, Jiang ordered the killing of about 5,000 Communists and any nationalists who disagreed with him.

Guangzhou was next on Jiang's list, and the **Communists** there knew that their time was up. By May 1927, Ho had to flee the city for Hong Kong, a small British colony on the southern coast of China. Ho wrote letters to his wife, but they never lived together again.

In the months that followed, Ho traveled around the world as an agent for the **Comintern.** He went back to Moscow, Germany, France, Italy, and then by ship to Siam (today known as Thailand). He used different names, wore disguises, and traveled on false papers. He was a wanted man, with the police only one step behind him. It was a desperate way of life, and he was often short of money and food.

However, Ho was sure that it was all worthwhile. **Communism** was on the rise, and **capitalism** seemed to be failing—just as Marx and Lenin had said it would. Even in London, at the heart of the powerful British Empire, **striking** workers were battling the government. In 1929, the economy of the United States collapsed overnight, starting a period of economic hardship called the **Great Depression.** It affected the whole world. Ho believed that even though the European powers had not been destroyed in World War I, surely failings in their own economic system would prove to be their downfall.

◀ *In 1927, military police in Shanghai arrest a suspected Communist.*

Troubled Times

Many people, both inside and outside Vietnam, were now working to end French rule there. Vietnamese **nationalists** had founded a new movement called the Viet Quoc in 1927. They wished to create a new **capitalist** state in Vietnam. The **Communists,** too, were gaining new recruits. Indeed, several different groups had formed. They included an Annam Communist party, an Indochinese Communist league, and a Communist party of Indochina.

Each had its own views on the way to proceed. How should they be allied to the Chinese Communist party? Should they start a **revolution** in Vietnam now or build up support for one later? Various groups tried to recruit one another's members. A rivalry also developed between the northern and the southern parts of Vietnam, too.

A new Communist party

Only one person was able to sort out the confusion—Ho Chi Minh. He could not reenter French Indochina, where the authorities wanted to arrest him. Instead, he traveled from Siam to Hong Kong, which had replaced Guangzhou as the chief center for Vietnamese **exiles** and **revolutionaries.**

Ho had always been good at dealing with people and getting them to work together. In Hong Kong, he addressed various concerns and looked for common ground among the representatives from the different Vietnamese groups. Together, in February 1930 these groups agreed to form a united Vietnamese Communist Party.

Later that year, word came from the **Comintern** in Moscow that the Vietnamese should change the name of the party to the Indochinese Communist Party. The name was meant to reflect the region as a whole. The change also wanted to show that Vietnamese independence was not the first aim of the party. This change revealed a lasting difference of opinion between Ho and Communist leaders in Moscow.

Storms in Vietnam

In Vietnam the **Great Depression** was having a huge effect. French businesses struggled and pulled their money from **plantations,** mines, and factories. Hardship was widespread.

In 1931–1932, both **nationalists** and **Communists** staged violent uprisings. Ho was pleased to see the French government in trouble in Vietnam. However, he was worried that the time had not yet come for a full **revolution.** He called for caution.

A Hong Kong prison

During the 1930s, police in all the **colonies** of Asia were on the lookout for troublemakers. Authorities arrested many rebels in Vietnam. On June 6, 1931, the Hong Kong police brought in Ho, who at the time was passing himself off as a Chinese citizen.

British authorities held Ho in prison but could prove no charges against him. This was a low point in his life. Jail was unpleasant, and the food was bad. He became sick. Police also

A most accomplished man

"A most accomplished man, speaking half a dozen European languages . . . a firm believer . . . that the pen is mightier than the sword."

(Press report at the time of Ho's arrest in Hong Kong)

arrested many of his personal and political friends, including his new love, Nguyen Thi Minh Kai. She was a Vietnamese Communist and a leading **campaigner** for women's rights. After their relationship ended, Nguyen Thi Minh Kai went to Moscow in 1934 and married another top Vietnamese Communist.

The British authorities wanted to **deport** Ho. After many arguments in courts in both Hong Kong and Great Britain, they finally released him in December 1932. Photographs of him at this time show a thin, worried-looking man whose face had begun to show signs of his hard life. And more troubles lay ahead.

▲ In the 1920s and 1930s, Ho was forever on the move, changing identity and in and out of prison.

Stalin's terror

Ho now traveled to Shanghai and then back across Siberia to Moscow, where he arrived in 1934. He found that the Soviet Union had changed greatly under Joseph Stalin's leadership. He had put many of the the original Russian revolutionaries on trial and imprisoned them. Stalin sent his chief opponent Leon Trotsky into **exile** in 1929. Beginning in 1928, Stalin had imposed agricultural reform in the face of strong opposition by the *kulaks* (land-owning peasants). He treated them brutally, executing many of them. Many people in the countryside were starving.

FOR DETAILS ON KEY PEOPLE OF HO CHI MINH'S TIME, SEE PAGE 58.

◄ *Stalin was **ruthless** and cruel, but the Soviet government portrayed him as a kind and wise leader.*

The secret police were everywhere, hunting down Stalin's opponents and imprisoning, torturing, or killing those they found. Some historians believe that Ho came under official investigation at this time.

Stalin disliked Ho personally, but Stalin still needed him as a future Soviet ally in Southeast Asia. Ho in turn needed Soviet support for his struggle to liberate Vietnam. At this point, no other country existed that could or would help.

While in the Soviet Union, Ho publicly claimed to support Stalin. He probably had little choice. If he had spoken out against Stalin's policies, authorities might have questioned his commitment to Communism and not supported his efforts to free Vietnam. In private, Stalin's policies must have concerned him.

Another way

Was there no other way forward for Ho? In the 1930s, another great colonial struggle was going on in India. Its leader, Mohandas Gandhi, was **campaigning** for freedom from British rule. Like Ho, Gandhi admired the traditional values of the farmers and villagers in his own country. However, Gandhi resisted British rule with nonviolent protest rather than revolution.

Ho believed that Gandhi could never bring about lasting social change because Gandhi based his political ideals on **spiritual** values—not economic facts. Nevertheless, Ho admired Gandhi greatly as a human being and as someone engaged in the same struggle. However, he himself still chose to follow the path of **revolution,** not reform.

► *Both Ho and Gandhi (center) struggled to liberate their peoples from rule by powerful empires. Gandhi (1869–1948) became known as Mahatma, which means "great soul."*

A disciple

"I and others may be revolutionaries, but we are all disciples of [Mohandas] Gandhi, nothing more, nothing less."

(Ho Chi Minh)

The World at War

It was 1938, and Ho—glad to be leaving Moscow—was on the move once again. From his train, he could see the dusty grasslands and cotton fields of central Asia streaming past the window. The **Comintern** had ordered him to return to China, but this time they told him to travel overland from Kazakhstan. He would cross China's western border and then travel to the city of Xi'an. From there, he headed south, walking, riding, on horseback, and lurching over rough roads on trucks. The whole country seemed to be on the move. China was at war with Japan.

TO LOCATE XI'AN, SEE THE MAP ON PAGE 30.

The war in China

Japan had occupied northeast China back in 1931, and it was now bombing cities and invading the rest of the country. Both Chinese **nationalists** and **Communists** resisted Japanese troops. Faced with a common enemy, they had to join forces. Where would the Japanese stop? It seemed that they were trying to control not just China but all of Southeast Asia.

Ho traveled under a false name, as usual. Everyone thought he was Chinese. He at last arrived in Guilin, an old city in southeast China, set in a beautiful countryside amid lakes, cliffs, and pillars of limestone rock. Traveling through this Chinese landscape must have made him think of the adventures he had read about as a boy in *Journey to the West*.

◀ In July 1937, Japanese troops captured China's capital city of Beijing.

In Guilin, Ho worked at the regional headquarters of the United Front (an alliance of Chinese nationalists and Communists), editing their journal and organizing public health facilities. He also wrote articles for a French-language Vietnamese newspaper called *Notre Voix (Our Voice)*, filing reports on Japanese **atrocities** in China and on the Chinese resistance. He later traveled further in China, reporting back to the Comintern in Moscow and making contacts. All the time, he kept in touch with the Communist rebels in Vietnam.

TO LOCATE GUILIN, SEE THE MAP ON PAGE 30.

France and Japan

From China, Ho followed the international news with great interest. In 1939, World War II (1939–1945) broke out in Europe. The **Nazi** party had come to power in Germany and was at war with Great Britain and France. At first Soviet leader Joseph Stalin signed a nonaggression pact (an agreement not to attack one another) with the Germans, but in 1941 Germany invaded the Soviet Union anyway.

The German invasion of France in 1940 greatly interested Ho. How would it affect Vietnam? The Germans set up a pro-German, French government in the town of Vichy, France. The so-called Vichy government took control of most of France's **colonies.** However, many French people in the colonies fled to set up anti-Vichy groups, fighting as the Free French.

In September 1940, the Vichy government agreed that Japanese troops could march into Vietnam, provided that the Japanese still allowed the French to run the country. Many Vietnamese nationalists welcomed the Japanese. The Vietnamese believed that because the Japanese were fellow Asians, they would eventually free the Vietnamese from their European masters.

Japanese gains, 1931–1937

Japanese gains, 1938–1941

SOVIET
UNION

MONGOLIA

Sea of
Japan

JAPAN

KOREA
(annexed
1910)

Beijing •

Xi'an •

• Shanghai

CHINA

N

W — E

S

• Guilin

• Kunming

TAIWAN

INDIA

Guangzhou •

PACIFIC
OCEAN

Hong Kong

BURMA

SIAM
(THAILAND)

South
China
Sea

PHILIPPINES

FRENCH
INDOCHINA

0   500 km

0   500 miles

▲ *During the 1930s and 1940s, Japanese troops swept through China and Southeast Asia.*

Ho warned against such ideas. Japanese invasion was not the answer to French rule, he declared, just part of the same problem.

9 The Vietminh

World War II made one thing certain. Now was the time for the Vietnamese to start their fight for freedom. In China, Ho and his followers began to set up a new secret force called the Vietminh. It aimed to unite **Communists** and **nationalists**—provided they were prepared to fight both the French and the Japanese.

Ho gave the new organization the official go-ahead at a conference of the Indochinese Communist Party in March 1941. Organizers held the meeting in an extraordinary place—a remote cave in the Pac Bo valley, just inside the Vietnamese border. Ho was there in person, for he had secretly crossed back into his homeland. He was roughing it, training new recruits and preparing for war. The Vietminh rebels had to dodge patrols of soldiers, and they would have been tortured and killed if they had been captured.

TO LOCATE PAC BO, SEE THE MAP ON PAGE 6.

At 50 years old, Ho was not as fit as the young rebels, but despite the danger and hardship, he was in good spirits. He was home again after 30 years. He earned the respect of the rebels, and it was during this period that people began calling him Ho Chi Minh, which means "bringer of enlightenment."

In December 1941, the Japanese bombing of Pearl Harbor, an American naval base in Hawaii, amazed Ho and his rebels. This meant that Japan and the United States were also now at war. Ho ordered the Vietminh operations in the north to spread to other parts of the country. He also began to wonder if the United States might not end up being a useful ally, now that Japan had become their common enemy.

Chinese prisons

Ho needed international support for the Vietminh. In the summer of 1942, he crossed back into China to seek backing from Chinese **nationalists** and **Communists.** However, authorities soon arrested him. Because Ho was carrying false identity papers, the police thought he must be a secret agent working for the Japanese.

Authorities transferred Ho from one jail to another. They kept him in grim conditions. He became sick with **tuberculosis.** Many months had passed before anyone realized the identity of this prisoner. Even then, the Chinese nationalists were far from eager to allow his release. More than a year passed before authorities gave him even limited freedom. He did not make it back to Vietnam until September 1944.

U.S. allies

In November 1944, a U.S. plane crashed in northern Vietnam. The Vietminh brought the pilot Rudolph Shaw to Ho's base at

◀ Serving with the Vietminh forces in the 1940s and 1950s, Ho became a man of action.

Pac Bo. Ho guided him to safety across the Chinese border, and they went on to Kunming in southern China.

TO LOCATE KUNMING, SEE THE MAP ON PAGE 30.

Kunming was the capital of the anti-Japanese alliance in China. Kunming was a weapons and supply depot for the British and Americans. The United States had many officials and soldiers stationed there. Ho met up with them several times and asked for help in their common fight against the Japanese.

Meeting the Americans

"The old man wears Chinese-type cotton trousers and buttoned-to-the-neck jacket . . . His little beard is silvery . . . his hair is still almost black. They [Ho and his colleague] both talk quietly but sometimes burst into chuckles. We seem to get on well together."
(Lieutenant Charles Fenn, U.S. Marines, describing his meeting with Ho in China in 1945)

Some Americans wanted to make contact with the Vietminh. These Americans could not give this organization their official backing because the United States still recognized France's claim to Vietnam. However, these Americans did provide a radio operator, medicines, and some weapons. They were suspicious of Ho's Communist connections, but they could not help but admire this ragged **revolutionary** who had walked in out of nowhere.

While Ho was talking to the Americans in China, World War II was coming to an end. The **Allies** had pushed Germany out of France, and the Free French now controlled Paris.

The final days

In Vietnam, a terrible **famine** struck, and the Japanese seized all the food they could find. They knew they were losing the war. In March 1945, the Japanese forced the French from power in Vietnam and handed the government over to the Vietnamese emperor Bao Dai. Though the Japanese still held the real power, that would not last long.

FOR DETAILS ON KEY PEOPLE OF HO CHI MINH'S TIME, SEE PAGE 58.

The Vietminh now sprang into action all over Vietnam. From May onward, Ho was back with the rebels, although he was often sick and feverish. The United States sent in a unit of troops to help, and Ho welcomed them.

August 1945

That August, Ho and his fighters heard by radio that the United States had dropped **atomic bombs** on two Japanese cities. Japan had surrendered to the United States, and the most terrible war the world had ever known was over.

In Vietnam, the long years of preparation and planning by Ho and by both **Communists** and **nationalists** soon paid off. With amazing speed, Vietminh forces took control of Hanoi, Hué, and even Saigon, where Ho's rebels were less well supported than in the north.

Before the French knew it, Bao Dai had given up the throne, and the Vietminh were in control of most of the former French **colony.** The Vietnamese declared independence on September 2. The new leader on the platform was none other than Ho Chi Minh, whom, as Nguyen Ai Quoc, the French had been chasing around the world for 26 years.

Return of the French

One major problem still existed for Ho's new Vietnam. France still claimed the country. Even though Germany had invaded and occupied France during World War II, the French were still not ready to agree to a free and independent Vietnamese state, especially one led by an old Communist enemy.

Communists and nationalists

In January 1946, Ho called a general election in all areas under Vietminh control. Many of the nationalists who had fought with the Vietminh did not want see a Communist takeover in their country. Against the wishes of many Communists, Ho proposed a **coalition government** (one in which the Communists shared power with the nationalists). It received a big vote of support.

Talks with France

Next, Ho needed to meet the French government. He and other representatives traveled to France for a conference. However, a change of government in France delayed the talks. This gave Ho time to relax and meet many ordinary French people. It was almost like a vacation—the first he had ever had. He was well liked by those who met him, who said he was charming and had a good sense of humor.

Talks finally began on July 6, 1946, but the new French government offered little. Ho did sign an agreement before he returned

▶ French prime minister Georges Bidault greets Ho before the Paris talks in July 1946.

TO LOCATE HAIPHONG, SEE THE MAP ON PAGE 6.

home, but in fact it was worth nothing. The French had already begun to bomb Haiphong, a major city and port on the Hong River delta.

A new war with France

In 1947, the French started to invade Vietnam all over again. As they reoccupied Hanoi, Ho and his government withdrew and launched a **guerrilla campaign** against them across the countryside. Ho's experience with the **Communist** troops in China had shown him how effective this kind of fighting could be.

By 1950, France was able to create a new state in the south. This state claimed to be an independent nation, even though the French firmly controlled it. The new Vietnamese president was the former emperor Bao Dai. France continued to fight in the north. It was a bitter war.

Key dates: Vietnam's war against France

1945	• Ho declares independence in Hanoi
1946	• Vietminh holds general election • Conference in France on the future of Vietnam
1947	• French troops invade Vietnam
1950	• French set up a new independent state in the south, with Bao Dai as president
1950	• First U.S. military advisers arrive in the southern state
1954	• Defeat of French troops at Dien Bien Phu The French leave Vietnam for the last time

The Cold War begins

Ho was still hoping the two countries could bring peace to Vietnam. However, as the war progressed, this did not seem likely. The **Cold War** had begun. It was a long period of political tension between **capitalist** and Communist countries. The Communist countries now included China, where Mao Zedong had defeated the **nationalists** in 1949.

The U.S. government believed that **Communism** was the enemy of **democracy**. The government thought it would spread throughout the world unless the United States stopped it. The United States believed that once one country went Communist, then its neighbors would follow. Because Ho was a Communist, the U.S. government saw him as part of this worldwide problem.

FOR DETAILS ON KEY PEOPLE OF HO CHI MINH'S TIME, SEE PAGE 58.

Strong roots

"Only when the root is firm can the tree live long,
And victory is built with the people as foundations."

(Poem by Ho Chi Minh, 1948)

▼ *After 1945, the Indochinese Communist Party divided regionally. Ho formed the Vietnamese Workers' Party (VWP). This photo shows him addressing the VWP National Conference in 1951.*

In fact, strong disagreements flared between the **Communist** countries. The Soviet Union, the world's most powerful Communist country, had by now little interest in foreign **revolutions,** except in cases where they would directly benefit the Soviets themselves. In 1950, Ho traveled to Moscow to meet Stalin, but the Soviet leader treated him with rudeness and scorn. Stalin considered Ho too moderate and too pro-Chinese.

Dien Bien Phu

The United States also wanted to make sure that precious supplies of natural **resources** from Southeast Asia, such as tin, **tungsten,** and rubber, would not be cut off. It set up a Military and Advisory Group (MAAG) in the southern Vietnamese state and provided 80 percent of the funding for the French war in the north. The United States shipped in **napalm** bombs that the French dropped from war planes. By 1954, the French had committed 250,000 troops to the colonial war.

FOR DETAILS ON KEY PEOPLE OF HO CHI MINH'S TIME, SEE PAGE 58.

Ho planned war policy carefully with his colleagues. But his military chief Vo Nguyen Giap was in charge of actual operations. The new government in China provided the army with food and weapons, but nobody outside Vietnam believed these ragged rebels could defeat the French army.

► *A French gun crew monitors a piece of artillery at Dien Bien Phu in March 1954. About two months later, the Vietnamese defeated the French and forced them out of Vietnam for good.*

The great Vietnamese victory came on May 7, 1954. The Vietnamese had finally defeated the French after eight weeks of fighting at Dien Bien Phu in the northwestern highlands. Ho's supporters, many of them women, had smuggled gun parts through enemy territory and carried them up mountain paths to positions above the French forts. The Vietnamese captured 10,000 French troops. The defeated French pulled out of Vietnam, and the war was suddenly over.

TO LOCATE DIEN BIEN PHU, SEE THE MAP ON PAGE 6.

This battle marked the end of French power in Southeast Asia. Ho had seen his dream come true after 35 years. Even so, he knew that the victory was a bitter one. The years of struggle had caused massive loss of life.

You will lose . . .

"You can kill ten of my men for every one I kill of yours, but even at those odds I will win, and you will lose."

(Ho, warning the French in 1946)

A Land Divided

With the French gone, Ho could now move back to Hanoi and set up the government of the **Democratic** Republic of Vietnam (DRV). He did this quietly, with little fuss. There were no victory parades.

He moved into a small, simple home on the grounds of a former palace that the government had taken over. Although the Vietnamese elected him president, Ho never approved of the kind of personal hero worship that Stalin encouraged in the Soviet Union. He preferred to see himself as part of a team and never forgot his simple village origins.

Bao Dai still controlled southern Vietnam, which was known as the State of Vietnam. Some northerners, opposed to Ho's government, fled south. Many of them were **Roman Catholics,** who feared that they would suffer in the north for following the religion of the old colonial rulers.

▼ *The former emperor Bao Dai (center, in pale suit) headed the State of Vietnam from 1949 to 1955.*

▲ *The Geneva Conference opened immediately after the French defeat in May 1954 and lasted into July. The **veteran** Vietnamese **Communist,** Pham Van Dong (front row, third from left), led the DRV delegation.*

The Geneva Conference

Ho knew that Vietnam would never find peace without international agreement over its future. The United States, the Soviet Union, France, Great Britain, China, Cambodia, Laos, the Democratic Republic of Vietnam, and the State of Vietnam all sent representatives to a peace conference in Geneva, Switzerland. Ho did not go to Geneva, but when he **briefed** the DRV team, he made it clear that they had to reach a realistic settlement.

The conference divided Vietnam temporarily into two parts and said that elections for a united country would be held no later than 1956. International authorities would supervise these elections to make sure that they were fair. No outside nation was to send troops into Vietnam or offer political backing to either the north or the south.

The United States had no intention of withdrawing its support for the south and did not sign the agreement. But the United States did agree not to challenge it by force. The other countries did sign the agreement. However, France then went against the agreement by declaring its support for the south.

The elections for a united country never happened. Year after year, Ho called for them to take place. But each time the United States, which was strongly opposed to **Communism,** claimed that this was just a plot by the DRV government. Little doubt existed that Ho would have won nationwide elections in the late 1950s.

Land reform

At home, the **Communists** were making enemies, even in the north. Most people saw Ho as a generally easy-going person, but many in his party were **hard-liners.**

The government introduced a program of land reform with the full support of Ho. The program aimed to give land back to the poorest people in society. Landlords and wealthy farmers, who owned most of the land, were against these changes. Between 1953 and 1956, the hard-liners followed the example of the Communists in China, using threats, torture, and execution to get their way. Ho condemned the violence and **atrocities,** which eventually stopped.

Foreign affairs

Ho was still popular, and in 1960 voters reelected him president of the DRV. He spent much of his time working on foreign policy. The international situation was changing fast. Stalin was dead, and the Soviet Union had a new leader in Nikita Khrushchev. Khrushchev had introduced reforms in the Soviet Union, but tensions with the United States were bringing the world close to **nuclear war.** A split grew between China and the Soviet Union, which Ho tried in vain to heal.

How to reunite?

The other problem that concerned Ho was **reunification** with the State of Vietnam. The number of U.S. military advisers there was growing rapidly. In 1955, the prime minister of the State of Vietnam, whose name was Ngo Dinh Diem, overthrew Bao Dai and became president himself after a **rigged election.**

FOR DETAILS ON KEY PEOPLE OF HO CHI MINH'S TIME, SEE PAGE 58.

By 1960, Ho was beginning to think that the State of Vietnam might collapse. Ngo Dinh Diem, a Roman Catholic, was unpopular. He had stirred up bitter opposition against members of non-Catholic religious groups, especially **Buddhist** monks. Buddhism was the most widely followed religion in Vietnam. To many **nationalists,** Christianity (the main religion in the State of Vietnam) was associated with French colonialism.

Ngo also persecuted **Communists.** Faced with jail or execution, they started to organize opposition in the south. They formed a movement called the National Liberation Front. Its fighters called themselves the People's Liberation Armed Force. They became widely known abroad as the Vietcong (short for *Viet Nam Cong San,* or Vietnamese Communists). Ho supported the Vietcong and offered them training.

▶ *Buddhist monks protest against President Ngo Dinh Diem in Saigon in August 1963.*

43

The Vietnam War

Ho was now in his 70s. His long life of hardship had taken its toll. His health was poor, and he looked frail. Younger people were gaining more and more power in the Democratic Republic of Vietnam, or North Vietnam. Many of them wanted to take on the State of Vietnam, or South Vietnam. However, many people still respected "Uncle Ho" (as he was known in the north), and he urged caution.

FOR DETAILS ON KEY PEOPLE OF HO CHI MINH'S TIME, SEE PAGE 58.

Ho knew that more and more U.S. troops were training soldiers in South Vietnam. Unrest grew there, too. In 1963, army officers overthrew and murdered the unpopular leader Diem. The new South Vietnamese leader was a general named Nguyen Cao Ky. He admitted that his personal hero was Germany's **Nazi dictator** Adolf Hitler.

All-out war

In 1964, two U.S. warships approached the coast of the Gulf of Tonkin, in North Vietnam. They were probably on a spying mission, testing out coastal defenses, and the North Vietnamese army fired upon them. This so-called Tonkin incident meant that the United States and North Vietnam were now openly at war.

Early in 1965, the Vietcong attacked a U.S. base in the south. U.S. warplanes started nonstop bombing of the north. Soon, the U.S. government had 200,000 troops stationed in South Vietnam. Later, Australia and New Zealand sent troops to join what became known as the Vietnam War.

The Vietnam War developed into one of the most brutal conflicts of modern times. **Communist** fighters and weapons passed from north to south down a secret route called the Ho Chi Minh Trail. U.S. planes destroyed cover by stripping

▲ *U.S. troops were fighting in harsh jungle conditions against a determined enemy.*

vast areas of jungle with a weedkiller called Agent Orange. U.S. and South Vietnamese troops set villages ablaze. Villagers burned to death with **napalm** sticking to their skin. The Vietcong, too, were **ruthless** fighters and executed many of their opponents, civilian as well as military.

Hero of the protests

Ho called upon international leaders to condemn the United States and the South Vietnamese forces. In Great Britain, France, Germany, the Netherlands, Scandinavia, Italy, Canada, Australia, and the United States itself, tens of thousands of demonstrators protested the war, often chanting the name of their unlikely new hero—"Ho-Ho-Ho, Ho Chi MINH!" The old rebel became world famous at the same time that he was losing power at home. Despite these protests, governments tended to side with their **Cold War** allies. Western European countries supported the United States, while Communist countries condemned U.S. actions.

It was the first time ever that television news had brought the cruel reality of modern warfare into the home. The violence shocked Americans, and public opinion soon became bitterly divided. More and more Americans turned against the war, and some refused to serve in the armed forces. However, while so many U.S. service personnel were being killed in action, other Americans harshly criticized the protesters for being unpatriotic.

Some international protesters made the journey to Vietnam and met Ho for themselves. He enjoyed talking to them. However, his health was failing. In 1965, he had to go to China for a long rest. Remembering his studies as a schoolboy, he visited the birthplace of the Chinese **philosopher** Confucius.

A letter to Lyndon Johnson

"Vietnam is thousands of miles away from the United States. But contrary to the pledges made by its representative at the 1954 Geneva Conference, the United States has ceaselessly intervened in Vietnam . . . The Vietnamese people will never submit to force . . . Our cause is absolutely just."

(From a letter sent by Ho, February 15, 1967)

The Tet offensive

By the beginning of 1968, the United States believed that they had almost won the war. However, Ho and the government of North Vietnam had been planning a major attack on the south. Ho finally ordered the attack to take place during Tet, the month of the Vietnamese new year.

About 67,000 combined North Vietnamese and Vietcong forces launched attacks on all major southern cities. Central Saigon became a battlefield. The forces destroyed 30 aircraft at the U.S. air base at Da Nang. In revenge for the Tet **offensive,** U.S. aircraft destroyed the city of Hué with bombs. The attack was not an overwhelming victory for the **Communists,** for they suffered heavy losses. However, it shocked the U.S. and South Vietnamese governments. They had not believed that such an attack was even possible. Many Americans were beginning to wonder if this terrible war could ever be won.

Ho, the **veteran** of so many wars, sensed at once that the Tet offensive marked a turning point. He felt like a younger man. He even tried to persuade his colleagues that he should travel secretly into South Vietnam, just as he had crossed over to Pac Bo during World War II. He wanted to inspire the men and women who were fighting, but he was now too frail to attempt such a mission.

▼ *Dressed in a cap and scarf and wearing glasses, 78-year-old Ho Chi Minh addresses villagers during a tour of North Vietnam.*

An Old Man Dies

Bombs fell on Hanoi, but Ho tried to find peace in his old age. He still lived in his simple home, tending his garden and feeding his goldfish. He received official visitors, and he advised the North Vietnamese government on policy. But he was no longer involved in everyday affairs.

War or peace?

FOR DETAILS ON KEY PEOPLE OF HO CHI MINH'S TIME, SEE PAGE 58.

In March 1968, U.S. president Lyndon Johnson had become weary of battling public opinion in the United States. He announced that he would resign from politics before the next election.

That May, the United States and North Vietnam at last agreed to peace talks. A conference began in Paris. Ho advised the government not to trust the United States completely but to work toward a settlement. However, no progress was made at the conference table, and the talks dragged on for four years, accomplishing nothing.

The United States elected Richard Nixon president in 1968. He had been a fierce critic of **Communism** since the start of the **Cold War.** Nixon reduced the number of troops in Vietnam but stepped up the bombing. He extended it into areas of neighboring Cambodia, where there had been support for the North Vietnamese and Vietcong forces since 1965. By April 1969, the Vietnam War had killed more than 33,000 U.S. soldiers. In North America and Europe, protests against the war grew ever louder. The war seemed to have spun out of control.

The last summer

On May 19, 1969, Ho celebrated his 79th birthday. His friends encouraged him, telling him that he would live to see victory.

However, during the long, hot summer, his health became much worse. He had chest pains and heart trouble. On the morning of September 2, 1969, after drinking some rice water, "Uncle Ho" had a sudden heart attack and died.

Radio Hanoi announced Ho's death on September 3. Vietcong forces in the south declared a three-day truce in his memory. World leaders, including many who were not **Communists,** paid him tribute. However, the United States and its **allies** did not praise their old enemy.

▶ *In 1969, Ho was still full of spirit and humor, but physically he was frail.*

The funeral

About 100,000 people came to the state funeral for Ho, 6 days after his death. The government held the funeral in Da Binh square in Hanoi, where he had declared Vietnamese independence in September 1945.

Ho had often stated that he wanted a simple **cremation** when he died. It would be healthier that way, he had said, and would save good land for farming. However, the government ordered his body to be **embalmed** instead, and seven years later they placed it inside a grand **mausoleum** overlooking Da Binh square. Vietnam's rulers wanted a glorious monument. The old man would not have approved.

▶ *Ho's admirers visit his mausoleum on Vietnam's National Day, September 2. This date commemorates both the Vietnamese Declaration of Independence in 1945 and his death in 1969.*

14 The World After Ho

Ho did not live to see Vietnam reunited. However, he was right to have seen the Tet **offensive** as a turning point in the Vietnam War.

In March 1972, units of the North Vietnamese army, numbering 120,000 men, invaded the south with the help of local Vietcong. The United States continued to bomb the north, but by 1973 President Nixon and his adviser Henry Kissinger realized that they could not win this war. The United States declared a cease-fire on January 27, 1973. Nixon called it "peace with honor," but to many Americans it seemed more like a defeat.

Ho Chi Minh City

South Vietnam fought on against North Vietnam in what was now a **civil war.** On April 30, 1975, South Vietnam surrendered to the north. Desperate Americans fled the U.S. embassy in Saigon by helicopter. Thousands of their Vietnamese supporters tried to escape with them.

The fall of Saigon brought to an end the struggle that Ho Chi Minh had started before World War I. The Vietnamese government renamed the capital city of the south, from which Ho had started his journey to Europe in 1911, Ho Chi Minh City in his honor.

A new nation

Vietnam was now a single country with a **Communist** government. However, old divisions still simmered. Many **nationalists** disliked the Communist government. Tension still existed between the mainly Communist north and the mainly nationalist south.

Many Vietnamese fled the country in search of a better economic life. Some of them escaped to Hong Kong and other Asian ports in leaky boats. Communities of Vietnamese **exiles** formed in the United States, Canada, Australia, and many other parts of the world.

The world moves on

However, over the years, the world changed. The Soviet Union collapsed in 1991, bringing an end to the **Cold War.** The Chinese government brought about **capitalist** reforms, though it still claimed to follow **Communist** policies. Vietnam, too, introduced reforms, made peace with the United States, and opened itself up to international trade. By the 1990s, Western tourists poured into Vietnam, and Da Nang became famous not for its air base but for its great surfing. This turned out to be the new world for which Ho laid the foundation.

▼ *Crowds and traffic throng the streets of Saigon, now officially called Ho Chi Minh City.*

Man of mystery

Although Ho was present at many of the great events of the last century, he remains a man of mystery. Perhaps this is because for much of his life he tried to keep hidden, changing his name and traveling in disguise. He had at least one marriage and several relationships but no family life. Politics was his world, but it is hard to find the private person beneath the public figure.

Looking back at Ho's life, there are many contradictions. He was a Communist who spent much of his life arguing with other Communists. He fought the French and yet spent some of his happiest days in France and was a lover of the French language. He was an admirer of the United States, and yet he became one of its greatest enemies.

Ho met many of the most important people of his day, but he himself lived in the simplest way possible, without riches, fine houses, or expensive clothes. He spent much of his life at war, and yet he longed for peace.

To many people in Vietnam and in other parts of the world, Ho is still an admired figure, who fought for freedom. Ho was not a power-hungry **dictator.** Most people who met him during his life, including some of his political enemies, found him to be a likable, friendly person.

The man who never gave up

Ho was, of course, single-minded. Politics drove him for 50 years. Any one of his **campaigns** would have exhausted most people. One reason Ho survived so long was his political cunning. He was always cautious, never in a hurry. He knew

▲ *Italian antiwar protesters carry pictures of Ho through the streets of Rome in 1967. His political ideas influenced a generation.*

when to talk and make a **compromise** and when to press forward with action. He was a realist, a natural "wheeler and dealer."

From 1919 onward, Ho attempted time after time to achieve a just settlement for his country through international **negotiation.** The bloodshed of the wars in Vietnam against France and the United States could have probably been prevented if the Western countries had to come to a peace agreement with Ho. They had chances in 1919, in 1945, in the late 1950s, and in 1964. But each time they ignored him.

A lifetime's struggle

"Without the cold and desolation of winter,
There could not be the warmth and splendor of spring:
Calamity has tempered and hardened me
And turned my mind into steel."

(Poem by Ho Chi Minh)

A place in history

It is sometimes said that people shape history. Ho would have disagreed. He would have declared that history is not made by individual people, but by whole classes of people as they react to the economic conditions under which they live.

Ho did not create the events that shook the world in his day, but he certainly took them on and faced up to them. Even those who disagree with his politics agree that in his struggle to change society, Ho was a tireless fighter and a remarkable man.

▶ *A statue of Ho looks across the city that now bears his name.*

Timeline

1890	Ho is born
1907	Attends the National Academy in Hué
1908	Support for protesting farmers leads to his expulsion from the academy
1911–	Travels around the world
1917	Finds work in Paris
1919	Forms the Society of Annamese Patriots in Paris
1923	Sails to the Soviet Union, works for the **Comintern**
1924	Travels to Guangzhou, China, to make contact with Communist revolutionaries
1927–	Vietnamese **nationalists** found the Viet Quoc
1930	Travels throughout Europe and Asia as a secret agent for the Comintern
	Forms the united Vietnamese Communist Party
1931	Uprisings by Communists and nationalists in Vietnam
1934	Returns to Moscow
1939	Travels in China for the Comintern
1940	Japanese troops enter Vietnam
1941	Vietminh forces founded
	Returns secretly to Vietnam

1942	Imprisoned in China on suspicion of spying
1944	Regains freedom and returns to Vietnam
1945	Vietminh campaigns throughout Vietnam Japan defeated Declares independence in Hanoi
1946	Vietminh holds general election
1947	French troops invade Vietnam
1950	French set up independent state in the south
1953–1956	Land reform in the north
1954	Defeat of French troops at Dien Bien Phu
1955	Bao Dai forced from power in South Vietnam
1956–1960	United States reject calls for joint elections
1960	NLF and Vietcong founded in South Vietnam
1963	United States sends troops to South Vietnam
1964	North Vietnam engages U.S. navy
1968	North Vietnam launches Tet offensive
1969	Ho dies at age 79
1975	South Vietnam surrenders

Key People of Ho Chi Minh's Time

Bao Dai (1913–1997) Bao was the son of the emperor Khai Dai and came to the throne himself in 1932, although real power remained with the French colonial government. Ho forced him from rule in 1945, but Ho kept him on as an adviser to the Vietminh government. However, Bao fled, only to return as president of the new French-backed southern Vietnamese state in 1949. Ngo Diem Dinh forced him from office in 1955, and he lived in exile in France.

Jiang Jieshi (1887–1975) Jiang (Chiang Kai-shek) was the Chinese general who fought to reunite his country for the **nationalist** Guomindang. He became party leader, ordering an attack on his **Communist allies.** He joined up with them again in order to fight the Japanese invasion, but in 1948, the Communists forced him from the mainland. He set up a rival Chinese state on the island of Taiwan.

Johnson, Lyndon (1908–1973) Johnson, the 36th president of the United States, had a strong interest in **social justice.** He became president after the assassination of John F. Kennedy in 1963. Although Kennedy had increased the U.S. presence in Vietnam, under Johnson it grew rapidly. As the war became ever more unpopular, Johnson took much of the blame. He once said that if he and Ho could ever get together, they could probably work out their differences. He retired from politics in 1968.

Lenin, Vladimir Ilyich (1870–1924) Lenin was a brilliant thinker and a shrewd politician who became a Communist activist and played the key role in the Russian **Revolution** of November 1917. Lenin saw the new Communist state through a bitter **civil war** and economic hardship.

Mao Zedong (1893–1976) Mao founded the Chinese Communist Party in 1921 and led a brilliant **guerrilla** campaign against both the Japanese and the Chinese **nationalists.** Mao provided the North Vietnamese with aid in their war with the United States.

Ngo Dinh Diem (1901–1963) A devout **Roman Catholic,** Ngo Dinh Diem became a successful government minister during the colonial period. In 1950, he left Vietnam, refusing to support either Ho Chi Minh or Bao Dai. With U.S. support, he returned to South Vietnam and became prime minister in 1954 and president the following year. He was unpopular and corrupt and a persecutor of **Buddhists.** He was overthrown with the support of the United States in 1963 and then murdered.

Nguyen Cao Ky (1930–) Having fought with the French against the Vietminh, Nguyen Cao Ky became an air force commander in South Vietnam and then president in 1965. He retired in 1971 and left Vietnam for the United States in 1975.

Stalin, Joseph (1879–1953) Stalin took part in the Russian Revolution of November 1917, in which the Communists overthrew the government. He gained power in the Soviet Union after 1924. Stalin was a **ruthless** leader who pushed through reforms even when they caused extreme hardship. He exiled, imprisoned, and murdered many of his opponents. He was a cunning international politician and played an important part in the Allied victory in World War II.

Vo Nguyen Giap (1912–) When Vo Nguyen Giap was a history teacher in Vietnam, he studied the military tactics used by the French leader Napoleon in the early 1800s. When the Vietminh was formed, he became their military chief. He built the small guerrilla force into an extremely effective army, which defeated the French at Dien Bien Phu in 1954.

Sources for Further Research

Allard, Denise. *Vietnam*. Chicago: Raintree Publishers, 1998.

Dudley, William. *The Vietnam War: Opposing Viewpoints*. Farmington Hills, Mich. Gale Group, 1997.

Duiker, William J. *Ho Chi Minh: A Life*. New York: Hyperion Books, 2001.

Gavin, Philip. *The Fall of Vietnam*. Farmington Hills, Mich.: Gale Group, 2003

Kalman, Bobbie. *Vietnam: The Culture*. New York: Crabtree Publishing, 2002.

Maga, Timothy P. *The Complete Idiot's Guide to the Vietnam War*. Indianapolis: Alpha Books, 2000.

Simmons, Pat. *Vietnam*. Chicago: Heinemann Library, 1998.

Uschan, Michael V. *The Fall of Saigon: The End of the Vietnam War*. Chicago: Heinemann Library, 2002.

Willoughby, Douglas. *The Vietnam War*. Chicago: Heinemann Library, 2001.

Zeinert, Karen. *The Valiant Women of the Vietnam War*. Brookfield, Conn.: Millbrook Press, 2000.

 Glossary

Allies, the group of countries—Great Britain, the United States, France, Australia, New Zealand, the Soviet Union, and others—that fought together in World War II against the Axis powers (Germany, Italy, and Japan)

allies countries (or people) who are on the same side and support each other in a conflict

atomic bomb a bomb in which a nuclear reaction takes place, creating a massive explosion

atrocities cruel or violent deeds

brief to give someone information or tell them about a plan of action

Buddhist a person who follows Buddhism, a religion of eastern and central Asia based on the teachings of the Buddha

campaign a program of activities or military action with a particular purpose

capitalism economic system based on private ownership of industry and resources

capitalist a word that describes an economic system based on private ownership of industry and resources

civil war war fought between rival groups in the same country

coalition government government formed when two or more political parties join and agree to work together

Cold War long period of political tension (1945–1991) between the United States and its allies, and the Soviet Union and China and other Communist countries

colonies countries ruled by another country

Comintern Communist International, an international workers' association founded in 1919

Communism political and economic system in which all property is owned by everyone

Communist someone who belongs to or believes in Communism, a political and economic system in which all property is owned by everyone

compromise when two sides reach an agreement by each giving up something they want or need

cremation burning of a dead body

democracy form of government in which supreme power is vested with the people

deport remove someone from a country

detain to hold someone and prevent their free movement

dictator ruler who does not allow ordinary people to have any say in how their country is governed

embalm to preserve a dead body by means of chemicals

exile someone who has been officially banned from his or her homeland

famine period of widespread and extreme hunger

Great Depression time of widespread business failures and job losses that began in 1929 and continued through the 1930s

guerrilla a type of soldier that fights in a small group, usually using small, surprise attacks

hard-liner someone who refuses to give up his or her opinion or change his or her policy

human rights the rights treated according to values that are common to all people, such as freedom from slavery

imperial relating to or suggesting of an emperor or empire

lobby to meet politicians or others in order to persuade them to do something

mausoleum tomb that is built as a grand monument

napalm flaming, jellylike substance used in bombs and flamethrowers to destroy the Vietnamese jungle

nationalist someone who believes that a country has the right to rule itself. In the struggles for self-rule in Vietnam and China, the term refers to nationalists who were against Communism.

Nazi member of the German National Socialist Workers' Party, a racist, violent, and antidemocratic political group that ruled Germany from 1933 to 1945

negotiation discussions to reach an agreed settlement

nuclear war warfare in which nuclear weapons of mass destruction are used

offensive attacking phase of a military campaign

parliament a group of elected leaders that makes a country's laws

patriot someone who loves his or her country

peace treaty the terms of settlement at the end of a war

philosopher someone who studies ideas and behavior

plantation large farm on which certain crops, such as rubber, tea, or sugarcane, are grown

prime minister the chief lawmaker in a parliamentary type of government. The office is similar to that of the president in the U.S. government.

resources country's wealth in the form of useful minerals, timber, water, etc.

reunification making a divided country into a single nation again

revolution complete change in the way that society is run. It may be brought about by the overthrow of a government.

revolutionary someone who supports a revolution or takes part in one

rigged election election in which the winner is chosen dishonestly

Roman Catholic belonging to the Christian group that is headed by the pope in Rome

ruthless having no compassion, pity, or mercy. Ruthless people will do anything to get their way no matter how much it hurts other people.

socialist somebody who supports public ownership and regulation of the economy in the interests of all

social justice the principle of fairness and equality

spiritual concerned with the world of the spirit, rather than the world of material things

stock share one of the units into which a company's wealth is divided in order to be bought and sold by the public

striking refusing to work until grievances have been met

tuberculosis infectious disease that affects the lungs

tungsten rare and valuable metal used in the manufacture of steel machine tools and lamp filaments

veteran someone who is experienced

warlord leader who uses military force to control a region of a country, opposing the authority of the central government

working class group of people in society who earn wages by laboring or making things

Index

32.79   32.79